Ivanka Trump:
More than just Donald Trump's daughter

Talia Rose

Dedicated to all the working mothers who are constantly trying to master the art of balancing work with parenthood.

©T. Rose Publications. All rights reserved. 2016

Table of Contents

1. Introduction
2. A short biography
3. The First Speech
4. An interview
5. Some Famous Quotes
6. Interesting facts
7. The Last speech
8. Conclusion

About the author

1. Introduction

Ivanka Trump is best known as the daughter of Donald Trump, the famous real estate mogul and presidential candidate. Unlike the children of many successful billionaires, she actually believes in hard work and has an impressive resume to show for it. An ex-model, designer, writer and a very successful business executive, Ivanka has a long list of accomplishments to her name. However, she took on yet another strong since June 2015 when her father announced that he is running in the Presidential race. In addition to giving numerous speeches and making public appearances alongside her father Donald, she has also become one of his most trusted advisers.

Even though, she projects herself as more of a businessperson rather than a politician, her role in the presidential campaign is second to none. She constantly supports and praises his father and also manages to keep him away from controversies. Over the coming months, she'll have to play more active and stronger roles to aide her father. Everyone will agree that a big part of Donald Trump's recent success as a presidential candidate has been and will be due to his exceptionally multi-talented daughter.

Without a further ado, let's jump into Ivanka's life story.

2. A short biography

Ivanka Marie Trump was born on October 30, 1981. Her father was the real estate developer and her mother was Ivana Trump a former model from Czechoslovakia. She was born and raised in New York. Her parents separated when she was only nine years old.

She got her bachelor degree in economics from the Wharton School and the University of Pennsylvania. She graduated with honors.

She has been greatly influenced by both of her parents. Her mother, the ex-model introduced her to glamour and fashion. Whereas, her father gave her the keys to the world of business. Ivanka's modelling career started in 1997 when she appeared on the cover of the magazine Seventeen. Since then, she has appeared on the covers of numerous magazines such as Harper's Bazaar, Golf Magazine, Forbes, Elle Mexico, Avenue etc. In addition, she was performed in fashion shows for famous brands such Thierry Mugler, Versace and Marc Bouwer. She also has her own line of bags, clothes, shoes and accessories.

Growing up in the lime light, Ivanka got accustomed to the media world from a young age. Her first TV appearance was in 1997 when she hosted the Miss Teen USA Pageant. In 2003, she was featured on the documentary "Born Rich". She appeared alongside her father on the 5th season of the TV show "the Apprentice" as a replacement for the regular co-host Carolyn Keptcher. Then Ivanka came back for the sixth season and also for the "Celebrity Apprentice."

Since 2009, she has been the Executive vice-president of real estate development and acquisitions of The Trump Organization. She is focused on the Trump hotels and fashion related business.

She started dating real estate developer a majority share holder of *The New York Observer* Jared Kushner in 2007 and the couple got married on October 25, 2009. Before getting married, Ivanka converted to Judaism which she still follows strictly. They have three children; Arabella, Joseph and Theodore.

3. The First Speech

When Donald Trump announced his candidacy for President of the United States on June 16, 2015, it wasn't his attractive wife Melania or one of his sons Donald Jr. or Eric who introduced him. It was his daughter Ivanka Trump. Her polished and elegant speaking style captured the heart of the audiences instantly. Here's the exact transcript of the speech.

Welcome everybody. Today, I have the honor of introducing a man who needs no introduction. His legend has been build and his accomplishments are too many to be named. That man is my father. Most people strive their entire lives to achieve great success in a single field. My father has succeeded in many; at the highest level and on a global scale. He has enjoyed success in a vast diversity of industries because the common denominator is him. His vision, his brilliance, his passion, his work ethic and his refusal to take no for an answer.

I've enjoyed the good fortune of working alongside my father for ten years now and I've seen these principles in action daily. I remember him telling me when I was a little girl, "Ivanka, if you're gonna be thinking anyway, you might as well be thinking big." And that's how he approaches any task that he undertakes. He thinks big. My father has employed tens and thousands of people throughout his career and he has inspired them to do extraordinary things. He has the strength to make hard decisions and to motivate those around him to achieve the impossible. He is an optimist who chases big dreams and sees potential where others do not. He leads by example and will outwork anyone in any room.

My father is the opposite of politically correct. He says what he means and he means what he says. He is also the best negotiator I've ever met. Countless times, I've stood by his side and watched him make deals that seemed impossible to get done. He has the discernment to understand what the other party needs and then to get exactly what he wants. May father knows how to be a fierce opponent, but also how to be a very loyal friend. When it comes to building bridges, he can do so figuratively, but also has the rare ability to do so literally on time and under budget.

Throughout his career, my father has been repeatedly called upon by local and federal government to step in and save long-stalled, grossly over budget public projects. Whether it's building a skating rink in the heart of central park, meticulously restoring the exterior façade of the Grand Central Terminal, enabling the development of New York City's Jacob Javits Convention Center, creating a championship public golf course for the city of New York or redeveloping the iconic but totally underutilized Old Post Office building on Pennsylvania Avenue in the heart of Washington D.C. my father succeeds time and time again where governments failed before him. I considerate myself fortunate to have learned from the best, both as an entrepreneur and as a parent. May father is a man who is deeply grounded in tradition. He raised my siblings and me to work hard and to strive for excellence in everything we do. He taught us that we have a responsibility to make a positive contribution to society.

Here today, my father is again leading me by example. My generation finds itself at cross-roads. Our leadership has been mired with bureaucracy of its own creation. If we don't adapt politically and economically, our country will be left behind. To address the many challenges we face, we don't need talk; we need action. We need execution; we need someone who is bold and independent. With a proven track record of successfully creating and building large complex and complicated organizations and in the process enabling many many Americans to better their lives. I can tell you that there's no better person than my father to have in your corner when you're facing tough opponents and making hard decisions. He is battle tested. He is a dreamer, but perhaps more importantly he is a do-er.

Ladies and gentlemen, it is my pleasure to introduce to you today, a man, whom I've loved and respected my entire life. My father Donald J. Trump.

4. An interview

In an intimate interview with CNN's Gloria Borger, Ivanka gave insights about her childhood and about her relationship with her father.

Here's the transcript of the interview. GB = Gloria Borger, IT = Ivanka Trump.

GB: *How would you describe your father as a parent growing up?*

IT: He was an incredible parent and is an incredible parent. But I think I appreciate it much more today as a parent of three young children. I think when I was a teenager I thought parenting is just something that just happens. Now I realize how much work goes into raising kids with a sense of purpose and work ethic. And raising them to be close to one another and obviously to stay close to their parents. I'm very grateful for him and my mother and all that they did for us as children and all that they continue to do for us today. But, he was the same type of parent as we see generally. He was funny.

GB: *Funny?*

IT: Sometimes wickedly so. Great sense of humor. He was demanding of us. He had very high expectations for us because he knew that we had the potential to accomplish. He saw the potential in us before we saw it in ourselves. And I think he really encouraged us to pursue our passions. He wanted us to find meaning and purpose in our lives. But he was very careful not to push us into real estate and I think that's partially because his excitement, his passion for real estate and everything he did, he brought home. And so I think we inherited a bit of his excitement and perhaps it's in the blood. But he always said to us "You have to do what you love. And you'll never succeed, you'll never compete at the highest level if you don't deeply love what you do. If you don't wanna get out of bed every morning and to do what it is you're doing." And he firmly believes that. It's probably the most consistent piece of advice he gave me my whole life. He would periodically check in with me and almost undermine my thought process about coming in to the family business because he wanted to make sure I knew that it wasn't an expectation of his.

GB: *So, when you're young. Was your dad the sort of dad who'd play games with you, read you bed time stories or different?*

IT: No, he was different. He wasn't long on diaper changing or things like that. I think he was a little bit more traditional in that regard. He was very accessible and very available. I think one of the things I think about most often is I never questioned that my siblings and I was his top priority. He never allowed us to; he never allowed us to question that fact because he always made us his top priority. So, it doesn't mean he was home every night for dinner; he wasn't. He was working very hard, he was building an enormous business. And he was in the early days of doing that when I was young and had a lot to prove to himself and to others and he had big ambitions for himself. He wasn't always physically present, but he was always available.

Actually as a little girl, a friend of mine reminded me of this recently. That she used to hang out with me in a janitor's closet where there was a pay phone at school. And at recess, I'd go there and I'd call collect to his office. I was probably ten years old. And I called collect to the Trump organization which is hilarious.

GB: *To say "Hi, this is Ivanka"?*

IT: And he would pick up the phone every single time. And he'd put me on speaker phone; wouldn't be a long conversation. He'd introduce me to whoever was in his office, but only in retrospect I love now; it didn't matter who was there. It was colleagues, it was titans of industry, it was heads of countries. He'd always take my call. He'd always tell everyone in the room how great a daughter I was and say cute things and he'd ask me about a test I took. But you know, I think that's really telling of him as a person and a parent. We always came first.

GB: *How about when you brought home a date and a boyfriend?*

IT: I was too smart to bring home a date or a boyfriend. I think I brought home my husband; that's it.

GB: *It's a little intimidating?*

IT: He was not my husband when I brought him home. I was not going to subject boyfriends to the scrutiny my father or mother for that matter. Unless I was a hundred percent sure.

GB: *And let me move on now to the campaign a little bit. Your father had said that you and Melania had wanted him to be more "presidential". Is that the word that he uses? Tell me about that. Because do you believe that the nick names he used for some people or the name calling was a mistake. Is that what you're talking about when you say more "presidential"?*

IT: You know my conversations with my father are really between us. Obviously, I'm his child and I've also been his colleague. I've worked alongside him for the past decade here at the Trump organization. And part of the reason we have such great relationship is because he respects me because I'm candid in my opinions and I share them; solicited or otherwise.

GB: *So, to that question, did you tell him those were mistakes?*

IT: Oh, once in a while he'd say things and I'd tell him he could probably do it ratcheting it back.

GB: *And he listens?*

IT: Sometimes. And sometimes he doesn't. Or sometimes he listens for limited periods of times.

GB: *But you can tell.*

IT: I think it's part of what people love about him. It's also part of what angers people. He is authentic and nobody tells him who to be. He is himself, he is his own man. He listens to the opinions of others; he respects the opinions of others. He processes the advice that people give him, but ultimately he makes his own decisions.

GB: *How do you reconcile the Donald Trump you know as your dad with the candidate that some people see and consider so divisive and how do you square that circle for our viewers?*

IT: My father has always elicited strong opinions in people. He is bold, he is unabashed, he is very himself. And I think for me, the most important thing is that I know the man. So when I hear things that are factually inaccurate, it's sometimes hurtful. I feel that as a daughter, but I still know the man. I as a woman, I as a person could never support someone who was sexist or racist. I just couldn't. I would not be able to be OK with that. But I know who he is as a human being and I know that those things aren't true. And not many people say those things and when they do, it's easier for me to dismiss it because of that fact.

5. Some Famous Quotes

Nothing demonstrates a person's personality better than his or her quotes and comments. Here are a few of Ivanka's best quotes:

"Real estate is my life. It is my day job, if you will. But it consumes my nights and weekends, too."

"I don't have a problem if somebody who has never met me wants to say that I wouldn't be where I was today without my family because you know what? They may be right. They probably are right. Who the hell knows? It's an impossible argument."

"In both business and personal life, I've always found that travel inspires me more than anything else I do. Evidence of the languages, cultures, scenery, food, and design sensibilities that I discover all over the world can be found in every piece of my jewelry."

"When you roll up your sleeves and set to work in a bunch of different areas, you can't help but help yourself."

"The more I work, the more I learn, the more I realize how much I still don't know."

"If people think I'm just the boss's daughter, they're deceived."

"You can be born into privilege, or you can not be born into privilege. You can be born into the opposite extreme and into poverty. I think from there on, though, you really do have to make your luck."

"In business, I believe that if you focus only on the journey, you'll miss the whole point of the enterprise. There has to be a goal, an end game of some kind; otherwise, you're just spinning your wheels. Yes, the journey is important, but the destination is important, too."

"I think it's the human condition to be frequently embarrassed by your parents."

"The harder you work, the luckier you get. I'm a big believer in that."

"I don't think you are truly successful unless you are a happy person and are happy with your life. I know many people who are professionally successful but miserable."

"I have always admired women that have a strong sense of self, complemented by femininity. I especially appreciate the presence of these women in traditionally male-dominated industries, such as real estate."

"I think my dad is highly gender-neutral. If he doesn't like someone, he'll articulate that, and I think it's also part of what resonates about him. He'll say what he's thinking."

"Pessimists are toxic. I love optimists - and by that, I don't mean people who are unable to see challenges. Optimists are solution-oriented."

"People ask me, do I ever disagree with my father? It would be a little strange if I didn't."

"Love what you do. There's always going to be someone else who's smarter than you, but there's no substitute for passion. People who are passionate always work the hardest, and that sets them apart!"

6. Interesting facts

Here are a few facts about Ivanka that a lot of people don't know.

She is Jewish: Ivanka converted from Christianity to Judaism in 2009 after studying with Rabbi Elie Weinstock before marrying real estate developer Jared Kushner. She only eats kosher and observes Sabbath.

She is a good friend of Chelsea Clinton: Even though their parents are on the opposite corners of the ring, the daughters were and still are very good friends. Chelsea said in a recent interview "Friendship always trumps politics and that's how it should be." They do have a few things in common; both of them grew up in the lime light, both of them have degrees from well reputed universities and they both are closely involved with their family businesses.

She worked for another organization before joining the family business: Instead of taking the easy way out and joining the Trump Organization right after graduating college, Ivanka. It was her professor Peter Linneman who recommended her to a position at Forest City Eneterprises, a development company in New York. That is where she first honed her craft for working in real estate.

7. The Last speech

Ivanka Trump speech at Republican National Convention on July 18, 2016 received countless praises. Here's the exact transcript of the speech.

Good evening. Thank you. One year ago, I introduced my father when he declared his candidacy. In his own way, and through his own sheer force of will, he sacrificed greatly to enter the political arena as an outsider.

And he prevailed against a field of 16 very talented competitors.

For more than a year, Donald Trump has been the people's champion, and tonight he's the people's nominee.

Like many of my fellow millennials, I do not consider myself categorically Republican or Democrat. More than party affiliation, I vote on based on what I believe is right, for my family and for my country. Sometimes it's a tough choice. That is not the case this time. As the proud daughter of your nominee, I am here to tell you that this is the moment and Donald Trump is the person to make America great again.

Real change, the kind we have not seen in decades is only going to come from outside the system. And it's only going to come from a man who's spent his entire life doing what others said could not be done. My father is a fighter. When the primaries got tough and they were tough, he did what any great leader does. He dug deeper, worked harder, got better and became stronger.

I have seen him fight for his family. I have seen him fight for his employees. I have seen him fight for his company. And now, I am seeing him fight for our country. It's been the story of his life and more recently the spirit of his campaign. It's also a prelude to reaching the goal that unites us all. When this party and better still this country knows what it is like to win again.

If it's possible to be famous and yet not really well known, that describes the father who raised me. In the same office in Trump Tower, where we now work together, I remember playing on the floor by my father's desk, constructing miniature buildings with Legos and Erector sets, while he did the same with concrete steel and glass.

My father taught my siblings and me the importance of positive values and a strong ethical compass. He showed us how to be resilient, how to deal with challenges and how to strive for excellence in all that we do. He taught us that there's nothing that we cannot accomplish, if we marry vision and passion with an enduring work ethic.

One of my father's greatest talents is the ability to see potential in people, before they see it in themselves. It

Hi Helen..

Just thought you might like to know more about Ivanka and Mrs. Trump.... Pass on to others..

Gloria

was like that for us to growing up. He taught us that potential vanishes into nothing without effort.

And like him, we each had a responsibility to work, not just for ourselves but for the betterment of the world around us. Over the years, on too many occasions to count, I saw my father tear stories out of the newspaper about people whom he had never met, who were facing some injustice or hardship.

He'd write a note to his assistant, in a signature black felt tip pen, and request that the person be found and invited to Trump Tower to meet with him. He would talk to them and then draw upon his extensive network to find them a job or get them a break. And they would leave his office, as people so often do after having been with Donald Trump, feeling that life could be great again.

Throughout my entire life, I have witnessed his empathy and generosity towards other, especially those who are suffering. It is just his way of being in your corner when you're down. My father not only has the strength and ability necessary to be our next President, but also the kindness and compassion that will enable him to be the leader that this country needs.

My father has a sense of fairness that touches every conviction he's hold. I worked alongside of him for now more than a decade now at the Trump Organization and I've seen how he operates as a leader; making important decisions that shape careers and that change lives.

I've learned a lot about the world from walking construction jobs by his side. When run properly, construction sites are true meritocracies. Competence in the building trades is easy to spot and incompetence is impossible to hide.

These sites are also incredible melting pots, gathering people from all walks of life and uniting them to work towards a single mission. There have always been men of all background and ethnicities on my father's job sites. And long before it was common place, you also saw women.

My father values talent. He recognizes real knowledge and skill when he finds it. He is color blind and gender neutral. He hires the best person for the job, period.

Words and promises, no matter visionary they sound will only get you so far. In our business, you're not a builder, unless you've got a building to show for it, or in my father's case, city skylines. Most people strive their entire lives to achieve great success in a single industry.

My father has succeeded in many on the highest level and on a global scale. One of the reasons he has thrived as an entrepreneur is because he listens to everyone. Billionaire executives don't usually ask the people doing the work for their opinion of the work. My father is an exception.

On every one of his projects, you'll see him talking to the super, the painter, the engineers, the electricians, he'll ask them for their feedback, if they think something should be done differently, or could be done better. When Donald Trump is in charge, all that counts is ability, effort and excellence.

This has long been the philosophy at the Trump Organization. At my father's company, there are more female than male executives. Women are paid equally for the work that we do and when a woman becomes a mother, she is supported, not shut out.

Women represent 46 percent of the total U.S. labor force, and 40 percent of American households have female primary breadwinners. In 2014, women made 83 cents for every dollar made by a man. Single women without children earn 94 cents for each dollar earned by a man, whereas married mothers made only 77 cents. As researchers have noted, gender is no longer the factor creating the greatest wage discrepancy in this country; motherhood is.

As President, my father will change the labor laws that were put into place at a time when women were not a significant portion of the workforce. And he will focus on making quality childcare affordable and accessible for all.

As a mother myself, of three young children, I know how hard it is to work while raising a family. And I also know that I'm far more fortunate than most. American families need relief. Policies that allow women with children to thrive should not be novelties, they should be the norm. Politicians talk about wage equality, but my father has made it a practice at his company throughout his entire career.

He will fight for equal pay for equal work, and I will fight for this too, right along side of him.

Americans today need an economy that permits people to rise again. A Trump Presidency will turn the economy around and restore the great American tradition of giving each new generation hope for brighter opportunities than those of the generation that came before. In Donald Trump, you have a candidate who knows the difference between wanting something done and making it happen.

When my father says that he will build a tower, keep an eye on the skyline. Floor by floor a soaring structure will appear, usually record setting in its height and iconic in its design.

Real people are hired to do real work. Vision becomes reality. When my father says that he will make America great again, he will deliver.

We have a chance this year, to reclaim our heritage as a country that dreams big and makes the impossible happen. Fortunately, Donald Trump is incapable of thinking small. When I was a child, my father always told me "Ivanka if you're going to be thinking anyway, you might as well think big". As President, my father will take on the bold and worthy fights. He will be unafraid to set lofty goals and he will be relentless in his determination to achieve them.

To people all over America, I say, when you have my father in your corner, you will never again have to worry about being let down. He will fight for you all the time, all the way, every time.

Maybe it's the developer in him, but Donald Trump cannot stand to see empty main streets and boarded up factories. He can't bear the injustice of college graduates who are crippled by student debt, and mothers who can't afford of the childcare required to return to work to better the lives of their families. Other politicians see these hardships, see the unfairness of it all, and they say I feel for you. Only my father will say, I'll fight for you.

The hard working men and women of this country identify with my father. He is tough and he is persevering. He is honest and he is real. He's an optimist and he's a relentless believer in America and all of her potential. He loves his family and he loves his country with his heart and his soul.

Politicians ask to be judged by their promises, not their results. I ask you to judge my father by his results. Judge his values by those he's instilled in his children. Judge his competency by the towers he's built, the companies he's founded, and the tens of thousands of jobs he's created.

He is the single most qualified serve as chief executive of an 18 trillion dollar economy. My father will call upon the best and brightest people from all spheres of industry and both side of the aisle. A new set of thinkers, to face our countries existing and future problems with fresh perspective and brave new solutions. Come January 17, all things will be possible again. We can hope and dream and think big again. No one has more faith in the American people than my father. He will be your greatest, your truest and your most loyal champion.

This is the fighter, the doer that you have chosen as your nominee, in ways no one expected; this moment in the life of our country has defined a mission and given it to an extraordinary man.

He is ready to see it all the way through, to speak to every man and every woman, of every background, in every part of this great country. To earn your trust and to earn your vote.

He earned that and much more from me a long time ago. I've loved and respected him, my entire life. And I could not be more proud tonight, to present to you and to all of America, my father and our next President, Donald J. Trump.

8. Conclusion

Ivanka Trump has proven again and again that she is more than the daughter of the famous Donald Trump. Her speech at the RNC was phenomenal and it clearly proved that she's in a league of her own. Even though both of them share the same last name, Donald and Ivanka are two very different person. The father is abrasive and over the top, whereas the daughter is more poised and always politically correct. Ivanka knows how to say the right things at interviews and hot go over hurdles smoothly. Unlike her flamboyant father, she is more down to earth and even her approach toward business is a lot more conservative.

She and her siblings are the next generation of Trumps who will lead the family business in their own styles. They might not be as controversial and over the top like their father, but we can be sure that they will take the family name even further with their millennial mentality.

I'd like to sign off with one of my favorite quotes form Ivanka. "You can be born into privilege, or you can not be born into privilege. You can be born into the opposite extreme and into poverty. I think from there on, though, you really do have to make your luck.

The End

If you've enjoyed this book, you'll also enjoy another one by the author.

Melania Trump: Everything you never wanted to know about America's future first lady

About the author

Born and raised in New York, Talia Rose has always been an avid reader since childhood. Hence, becoming a writer was the natural path for her to take. She has an open mind and is always ready to learn from the inspiring stories of others. Besides her daily trips to Starbucks and the strolls down Central Park, her most favorite activity is to entertain her readers through her writings.

Made in the USA
Lexington, KY
29 January 2017